Comptroller of the Currency
Administrator of National Banks

Installment Loans

Comptroller's Handbook
(Section 209)

Narrative - March 1990, Procedures - March 1998

Assets

Installment Loans
(Section 209)

Table of Contents

Introduction	1
Organization of Bank Department	1
Lending Policies	2
Classification of Credits	3
Repossessed Property	5
Insurance	5
Loan Approval Methods	5
Indirect Loans	6
Violations of Law	8
Examination Procedures	9

Installment Loans
(Section 209)

Introduction

A bank's installment loan portfolio is usually comprised of a large number of small loans, each scheduled to be amortized over a specific period. Most installment loans are made directly for consumer purchases, but business loans granted for the purchase of heavy equipment or industrial vehicles, such as tractor-trailers or buses, may also be included. In addition, the department may grant indirect loans for the purchase of consumer goods.

Organization of Bank Department

The installment loan department is normally divided into four basic functional areas: acquisition, servicing, payment processing, and collection. The acquisition area originates the loan, which includes direct contact with the customer or dealer, the gathering and review of credit information, and the decision to grant or reject the loan. Servicing includes disbursing loan proceeds, processing loan forms, preparing payment books, controlling notes, collateral and documentation, and preparing various reports, such as delinquencies, extensions, renewals, and irregular payments. The payment area handles the collection, processing, and posting of all payments received by the bank. The collection area provides the follow-up, adjustment, and other related activities involved with delinquent loans.

Installment loan departments in larger banks may have divisions for different types of loans. The specific breakdown will vary from bank to bank, but may include divisions specializing in direct consumer loans, indirect loans, small business loans, fleet leasing loans, indirect leasing loans, equipment financing, and education loans. The functional duties within one division may be consolidated with similar functions of other divisions. Thus, in a particular bank, the acquisition function may be handled by type of loan, and the remaining functions may be consolidated.

The examiner must determine the organization of duties and responsibilities within the department at the start of the examination. That helps to insure a smoother flow of information from bank personnel to the examiner and aids in ensuring that all areas of the department are considered in the examination.

The installment loan department may be responsible for other types of loans.

The most common of those are floor plan loans, credit card plans, and check credit plans. Those loans are covered in separate sections of this handbook.

Since installment loan departments handle a large volume of loans, most banks use automated systems. The data and schedules needed by the examiner will normally be generated by the system as a routine matter since they are also required by department personnel. Management Information System (MIS) reports will probably be the major source of detailed information concerning each loan. These reports should include the following information: renewals, extensions and deferrals, past-due, charge-offs, and collection efforts. Any lack of that information may constitute a serious shortcoming within the department.

In those banks that do not use automated systems, the necessary schedules should still be routinely prepared. The examiner should request their preparation and test their accuracy.

The examiner's emphasis in reviewing the installment loan department should be on the overall procedures, policies, and credit qualities. His or her goal should not be limited to identifying current portfolio problems, but should include potential future problems that may result from liberal policies, unfavorable trends, potentially dangerous concentrations, or non-adherence to established policies.

Lending Policies

In addition to the policy guidelines detailed in the loan portfolio management section of this handbook, bank management should have established procedures to identify and monitor unfavorable trends. Past-due percentages and income and loss trends must be monitored closely. Unfortunately, in banks that lack a well-enforced charge-off program, loss ratios are often meaningless for periods of less than a year. As a result, bank management may not become aware of downward trends until year-end or until examiner initiated charge-offs are made. That delays recognition and implementation of any necessary corrective action. Therefore, the examiner should determine that an automatic charge-off procedure has been adopted. Review should be limited to ascertaining that exceptions meet established guidelines.

In cases for which no specific charge-off procedures have been established, or where adherence to the established procedures is found to be lax, every effort should be made by the examiner to encourage the bank to adopt and follow acceptable procedures. The absence of a specific charge-off policy will necessitate the review of small overdue loans with management. The review should precede any work required on specific loans selected for analysis, and can usually be accomplished from the computer generated delinquency reports for banks where supervision and authority is vested in one or two individuals. In banks where contact with numerous offices or officers is necessary, discussion of delinquencies should be delayed until a determination is made of other credits necessitating discussion.

When reviewing the installment lending area, the following are some of the danger signals that can indicate inherent policy weaknesses:

- Granting the obligor continuous extensions or rewrites to correct chronic delinquencies.

- Financing the full purchase price. The customer should have some equity in the goods to show good faith.

- Financing contracts with balloon payments that materially lengthen the indicated maturity.

- Weak collection policies in the early stages of delinquency.

Classification of Credits

Delinquent installment loan paper should be classified as follows:

- Substandard -- Consumer installment paper delinquent 90-119 days.

- Loss -- Consumer installment paper delinquent 120 days or more.

Below is an example of paper delinquent 90-119 days and paper delinquent 120 days or more.

EXAMPLE

Due Date	Period	Delinquency Status*	Comments
3/10	3/11-04/09	Not delinquent	---

4/10	4/10-05/09	30 days or 2 payments	OCC considers delinquent
5/10	5/10-06/09	60 days or 3 payments	---
6/10	6/10-07/09	90 days or 4 payments	Substandard
7/10	7/10-08/09	120 days or 5 payments	Loss

* A payment equivalent to 90 percent or more of the contractual payment may be considered a full payment in computing delinquency.

The following loans are subject to this classifications policy:

- All loans to individuals for household, family, and other personal expenditures as defined in the Instructions for the Preparation of Reports of Condition.

- Mobile home paper, with the following exception:

    When applicable state laws define the purchase of a mobile home as the purchase of real property, and the loan is secured by the purchased mobile home as evidenced by a mortgage or similar document.

- Federal Housing Authority (FHA) Title 1 loans. Those loans are also subject to the following classification criteria:

    - Uninsured portions should be charged off when claims have been filed.

    - When claims have not been filed, uninsured delinquent portions should be classified in accordance with the delinquent installment loan classification policy.

    - The portion covered by valid insurance is not subject to classification.

Exceptions to this classification policy may occur, particularly when significant amounts are involved and the bank can demonstrate that repayment will be made irrespective of delinquency status. Alternatively, those policies do not preclude the classification of assets delinquent for a lesser period when classification is warranted.

Delinquent business installment loans that are subject to classification may be detailed at the discretion of the examiner.

The above guidelines must be observed on small, delinquent installment credit loans, and they may be listed as loss in the report of examination without detailed comments.

Repossessed Property

Repossessed property should be booked at the lower of the recorded investment in the loan satisfied or its fair market value on the date the bank obtains clear title and possession of the property. Any excess of the recorded investment in the loan satisfied over fair value must be charged against the allowance for loan and lease losses. Periodic repricing should be performed and further write-downs taken as necessary to reflect the current market value. Additional write-downs as a result of repricing are not charged against the allowance for loan and lease losses, but accounted for as an expense of owning repossessed property.

Generally, repossessed property should be disposed of within 90 days of obtaining possession, unless legal requirements stipulate a longer period.

Insurance

Credit life insurance is term life insurance coverage on individual borrowers. Under this type of protection, if the obligor dies, the bank's loan is repaid from policy death benefits, rather than from the estate. Some banks have skip insurance and other types of coverage. The examiner should inquire about the various insurance coverages in effect and should review the policies for the amount and type of coverage and the expiration date.

Loan Approval Methods

Management's objective in the loan approval process is to balance growth with the level of risk taken into the installment loan portfolio. Banks use two basic methods for determining creditworthiness: judgmental and credit scoring. In both cases, the profiles of past borrowers are compared with those of current applicants. The profiles are used as a basis for predicting the likelihood that a new borrower will have a good or bad account if the application is approved.

Using the judgmental method, every application is reviewed by a bank loan officer or a credit analyst. Based on training and experience, the loan officer or analyst attempts to predict the likelihood that the applicants will be good or bad credit customers.

The credit-scoring method distinguishes between potential borrowers by comparing the information on their application to borrower profiles drawn from the bank's lending experience using advanced statistical methods. Applications that score above the bank's cutoff score would ordinarily be approved. From management's perspective, a properly established credit- scoring system reduces the likelihood of discrimination in the granting of installment credit. Credit-scoring also enables management to assess more precisely the consequences that different approval policies (i.e., changes in the cutoff score) carry for the level of risk taken into the installment loan portfolio.

Indirect Loans

Indirect loans are granted elsewhere and subsequently purchased by the bank. They arise most frequently when a dealer has sold inventory on an installment basis and, subsequently, discounts the buyer's obligation to the bank. Because the loan is not originated by the bank, the banker must determine that the loan is an acceptable credit risk, and that a bona fide transaction has occurred to support the evidence of debt being taken into the bank's loan portfolio.

Dealer relationships should be governed by a detailed, written dealer agreement. Topics that should be included are acceptable types of merchandise, credit requirements for borrowers, maximum advance and repayment terms, discount rate, recourse agreement, and reserve requirements.

There are three different types of recourse that a dealer may provide on indirect loans that have been discounted to the bank. The type of recourse may affect ultimate collectability should the indirect loans become delinquent. Under a full recourse agreement, the dealer must repurchase the loan at the bank's demand. With limited recourse, the dealer may be obligated to repurchase the loan or repossess the goods if the bank fulfills certain obligations. Without recourse, the dealer has no obligation on the loan unless fraud or misrepresentation was involved. The bank should be requiring current credit information on all dealer discounted loans. The need for financial information on the dealer depends on the level of support expected from the dealer. Certainly, current financial statements should be on file for all dealers discounting any form of with-recourse paper

In addition to the possible profit derived from the sale of the property, the dealer usually makes an additional profit on credit-sale transactions by charging a higher rate to his customer than that required by the bank. The difference between the two rates, called dealer's differential, might not be paid to the dealer at the time the contract is purchased by the bank. The dealer's agreement may require that a portion of the differential on each contract be placed in a separate deposit account under the control of the bank. The funds accumulated in that account are commonly known as a dealer's reserve account.

Dealer's reserve accounts may be used by the bank to assist in refunding interest on prepaid contracts, and to offset losses on contracts on which the dealer is obligated, but has failed, to perform. The dealer's agreement will specify the maximum limit for such reserves and the terms under which refunds may be made to the dealer. If a high proportion of the contracts prove to be of good quality, with few losses, the reserve will grow to exceed the required limits and the excess may be paid to the dealer. Such refunds serve as a profitable incentive to the dealer to produce sales contracts of high quality. If no reserves are required by bank policy, the incentive to produce good sales contracts is replaced by the incentive to produce a high volume of contracts, without regard to quality, for the immediate profit comprising the dealer's differential.

Holdback reserves are similar to dealer's reserve accounts. A holdback is usually a stipulated portion of a contract, rather than a mere portion of the dealer differential. Holdbacks occur primarily on those contracts the banker believes represent a risk greater than should normally be accepted from the dealer and represent a departure from sound lending practices.

The adequacy of a dealer's reserve account depends on a number of factors, including types of purchasers, types of collateral, and delinquency and repossession experience. In some areas, dealer holdbacks and dealer's reserves have disappeared, along with recourse endorsements, as a requirement for discounted paper.

To determine the condition of the indirect portfolio, the examiner may review past-due loans and total outstandings by dealer, charge-off reports, collection reports, and reports of extensions, deferrals, and renewals.

The following are some danger signals that may be present in the indirect loan portfolio. (1) The dealer, instead of the bank, accepts the borrower's payments, leaving the bank with less control over the loan. (2) The dealer makes payments on behalf of the borrower, perhaps disguising past-due accounts. (3) The purchaser is allowed to apply for the title, possibly resulting in an improperly recorded lien. (4) The dealer finances the borrower's down payment, permitting the borrower to have no stake in the collateral property. (5) Permitting or initiating overdrafts in the dealer reserve or holdback accounts, capitalizing losses that are to be paid from future business. (6) Placing full reliance on the dealer for credit checking. (7) Financing either a dealer or his discounts, which are out of the bank's normal trade area.

Violations of Law

The installment loan department is particularly susceptible to violations of the various consumer credit laws and regulations, which may result in serious financial penalties and loss of public esteem. Therefore, the examiner must be aware of any violations discovered during the consumer compliance examination and ensure that corrective action has been effected. All examiners should be familiar with the various consumer credit laws and regulations and be alert to violations during the examination of this department.

General Procedures

These procedures are intended to determine the adequacy of the bank's policies, procedures, and internal controls as they relate to Installment Lending. The extent of testing and procedures performed should be based upon the examiner's assessment of risk. This assessment should include consideration of work performed by other regulatory agencies, internal and external auditors and other internal compliance review units, formalized policies and procedures, and the effectiveness of internal controls and management information systems (MIS).

Objective: Determine the scope of the examination and identify examination activities necessary to achieve stated objectives.

1.   Review the following documents to identify any previous problems that require follow-up.

    ☐ Supervisory strategy in the OCC's Electronic Information System.
    ☐ EIC's scope memorandum.
    ☐ Previous Report of Examination.
    ☐ Working papers from the previous examination.
    ☐ Audit reports, and working papers if necessary.
    ☐ Correspondence memorandum.
    ☐ Loan review reports.

2.   From the EIC, obtain the results of his/her analysis of the UBPR, BERT, and other OCC reports. Identify any concerns, trends, or changes in installment lending.

3.   In addition to general information requested in LPM, obtain and review internal reports management uses to supervise installment lending. Some examples include:

    ☐ Installment delinquencies, repossessed assets, charged-off loans.
    ☐ The bank's current installment business and strategic plans.
    ☐ The budget for installment lending at the beginning of the year, and

budget revisions as of the examination date.

- [ ] An organization chart including each functional area.
- [ ] Copies of formal job descriptions for all principal installment lending positions.
- [ ] Resumes of principals in the department.
- [ ] Copies of management compensation programs, including incentive plans.
- [ ] Copies of any board reports concerning installment lending operations since the last examination.
- [ ] Copies of key management reports used by department management.
- [ ] Copies of all installment lending internal and external audit reports and loan review reports since the last examination, and copies of any management responses.
- [ ] A list of board and executive or senior management committees that supervise installment lending, including a list of members and meeting schedules. Also obtain copies of minutes documenting those meetings since the last examination.
- [ ] A summary listing of all installment products (including indirect loan products) offered and a brief description of their characteristics, including pricing.
- [ ] Copies of marketing plans for the installment lending department overall and by product.
- [ ] Copies of loan policies and procedures for all installment lending products.
- [ ] A list of scoring systems in use and copies of their manuals. Also obtain a list of credit bureaus used as well as a description of any credit bureau scoring that is used.
- [ ] A list of installment securitizations and copies of the prospectus' associated with those offerings.
- [ ] A balance sheet and income and expense statement for the installment lending department as of the examination date and most recent year-end.

4. Obtain loan MIS reports, as needed:

- [ ] Summary reports showing trends in outstandings, new volume, delinquencies, losses, and new loan and portfolio yield by the different installment product splits (e.g., new car, used car, recreational vehicle, truck, boats, etc.)

- ☐ Credit scoring distribution reports by portfolio, new volume, delinquencies, and losses.
- ☐ Direct and indirect trial balances.
- ☐ Dealer analysis/efficiency reports showing number of applications, applications approved and booked, percentages of approved and booked, new dollars of loans booked, portfolio balance, delinquency and losses.
- ☐ Balances of dealer reserves or holdback accounts.
- ☐ Past-due reports.
- ☐ Extensions and renewal reports for the latest month-end and previous month-end summaries.
- ☐ Loans with irregular or balloon payments.
- ☐ Loans with more than five prepaid installments.
- ☐ Loans generated by brokers or finders, including the terms of applicable credit enhancements or recourse.
- ☐ Loans charged off since the previous examination including all information necessary to prepare the IRS express determination letter (charge off between examinations form).
- ☐ Current repossession information including:
  - – A description of the borrower.
  - – The estimated value of the item repossessed.
  - – Date of the repossession.
  - – Date on which the bank obtained title to repossessed property.
  - – The balance outstanding.
  - – Repossession deficiency balance analysis (helps gauge the effect on losses of the amount borrowed after the down payment.

5. Obtain the following from either the examiner performing LPM or the bank EIC:

- ☐ Any useful information obtained from the review of minutes of the loan and discount committee or any similar committee.
- ☐ Reports related to installment lending that have been furnished to the loan and discount committee or any similar committee, or the board of directors.
- ☐ List of directors, executive officers, principal shareholders, and their interests.

6. Verify the completeness of requested information with the request list.

7. Determine, during early discussions with management:

    - Any significant changes in policies, practices, personnel relating to activities, systems, loan approval or collection processes.
    - Material changes in products, volumes, and changes in market focus.
    - Levels and trends in delinquencies and losses for each loan type.
    - Any internal or external factors that could affect installment lending operations.

8. As procedures are performed, determine whether bank officers are operating in conformance with established guidelines.

9. Based on the performance of these steps and discussions with the bank EIC, determine the scope of this examination and its objectives.

    Note: Select steps necessary to meet objectives from among the following examination procedures. All steps are seldom required in an examination.

Quantity of Risk

Conclusion: The quantity of risk is (low, moderate, high).

Objective: To determine the quantity of risk relative to installment lending, including an evaluation of the portfolio for collateral sufficiency, credit quality, and collectability.

1.   Evaluate the reasonableness of management's business and strategic plans for the department. Consider the following:

   - Are they clear?
   - Do they reflect the current department's direction?
   - Are they consistent with overall bank objectives?

Department Performance

1.   Evaluate the installment lending department's performance by conducting the following:

   - Obtain a profitability report for the department and compare actual performance to budget.
   - Review bank product profitability and loan pricing models to determine proper income and expense allocations.
   - By using management reports and the UBPR, review management's and the department's performance by analyzing:
     - Profitability trends.
     - Delinquency trends.
     - Loss and recovery trends.

2.   Discuss adverse trends and large or unusual variances to budget with management.

Underwriting

1.   Assess the level of credit risk for all new products implemented since the last examination, and to the extent possible, those planned products. Consider:

- Reasonableness of underwriting guidelines.
- Performance of product types.
- Volume and significance of exception levels.
- Compliance with laws, rulings, and regulations.

2. Evaluate the level of risk in the bank's credit scoring systems or other criteria used for credit underwriting. If scoring systems are used, determine the following:

    - How they were developed.
    - Whether they are monitored.
    - Whether they are periodically revalidated.
    - Whether they rank risk effectively.

3. If credit scoring is used, evaluate the level of risk associated with the score care by:

    - Reviewing the underlying documentation used to developed the score card.
    - Evaluating how the cutoff score and decision criteria were established.
    - Comparing the cutoff score to the "odds" table to determine the level of risk being taken (the higher the odds, the lower the risk).
    - Evaluating the added risk of any decrease in the cutoff score (i.e., risk increases as the cutoff score decreases).

4. If the bank engages in "pre-approved" lending, evaluate the level of risk associated with different methods of soliciting new business.

Testing

For installment lending, there are detailed testing procedures for four areas; underwriting practices, score model overrides, loan renewals and extensions, and MIS. Prior to performing any testing procedures, you will need to determine which areas require thorough examination. All tests do not necessarily need to be performed at each examination. Deciding which tests are needed depends on the individual bank's risk profile and the scope of their installment lending activities.

1.   Identify which installment lending tests need to be performed. Consider the following:

- The risk profile of the bank to include the following:
  - Areas of risk identified during the last examination.
  - Areas of risk identified during the performance of the general procedures.
  - The scope of the bank's installment lending activities.
  - The types of products offered.
- Any significant changes in underwriting practices.
- The volume of scorecard model overrides.
- The volume and frequency of loan renewals and extensions.
- The quality and adequacy of MIS.
- The volume of indirect lending activities.
- The level of asset securitization practices.
- Areas of risk identified by the Loan Review and Audit functions.
- Input from the bank EIC.

2.   Perform the following procedures for the areas of risk identified.

Underwriting practices

1.   Pull a sample of new loans booked in the past 30-180 days as follows:

- Select loans from a current trial balance, using a numerical statistical sampling technique.
- Depending on the bank, the audit department may be able to help select a sample using their software.

2.   Set up a worksheet to include the following testing criteria:

- Policy guidelines.
- Underwriting terms.
- Collateral documentation requirements.
- Pricing information.

3.   Conduct the file review by transcribing the worksheet information from credit files, automated systems, and/or MIS reports.

---

4. During your sample review, evaluate the quality of underwriting practices by determining the following:

    - Compliance with policy guidelines, including credit criteria, documentation, pricing, terms, etc.
    - The credit quality of new loans and whether the quality has changed since the last examination.
    - The volume (number and size) and significance of approved policy exceptions.
    - Level of classified/criticized loans.

Score model overrides

1. Pull a sample of new loans booked in the last 30-90 days, that scored below the "cutoff" but were approved anyway, as follows:

    - Select loans using a numerical statistical sampling technique.
    - For selecting sample loans, use reports related to the test.
    - In some banks, the audit department may be able to help select a sample using their software.

2. Set up a worksheet to include the following testing criteria:

    - Policy override guidelines.
    - Reason(s) for the override.
    - Appropriateness of the credit decision.

3. Conduct the file review by transcribing the worksheet information from credit files and/or other applicable reports.

4. During your sample review, determine:

    - Whether the reason for the score override is documented.
    - Compliance with override policy requirements.
    - The appropriateness of the credit decision.

Loan renewals and extensions

1.   Pull a sample of loans as follows:

   - From the entire population to test usage and accuracy of reporting.
   - From the renewal and extension listing to test compliance with policy.

2.   Set up a worksheet to include the following criteria:

   - Loan renewal and extension policy guidelines.
   - Number of extension(s)/renewal(s)
   - Justification or support for the decision(s).
   - Accuracy of reported information.

3.   Conduct the file review by transcribing the worksheet information from credit files and/or other applicable reports.

4.   During your sample review, determine:

   - Compliance with renewal/extension policy requirements.
   - The degree of usage.
   - The appropriateness of the decision.
   - The accuracy of the reported information.

MIS

1.   During the various testing procedures, verify the accuracy of MIS by:

   - Tracing reportable items to appropriate listings/reports including past dues, renewal and extensions, prepayments, and insider loans.

Testing Summary

1.   For all testing performed, consolidate exceptions and any unusual patterns identified.

Indirect Lending

1.   Evaluate the adequacy of indirect lending guidelines and the underwriting guidelines used to purchase loans generated by dealers.

2.	Obtain management's internal risk ratings of dealers.

3.	Evaluate the overall quality of indirect lending by reviewing dealer summary reports for information on outstanding loans, new volume, delinquencies and losses, outstandings with recourse, and floor plan financing and other loan relationships. Consider:

-	The volume of large dealer relationships.
-	Any significant increases or decreases in volume.
-	The level and volume of trends in delinquencies and losses.

4.	Determine whether a financial analysis of any dealers needs to be done by looking at:

-	Loan volume and outstandings.
-	Levels and trends in delinquencies and losses.
-	Outstandings with recourse.
-	The bank's risk ratings.

5.	Select dealers for review. Coordinate any financial review with examiners performing floor plan financing and other loan program reviews. The review should assess:

-	The financial condition of the dealers.
-	Compliance with loan policy.
-	Compliance with the dealer agreement.
-	The accuracy of the bank's risk rating.

6.	Review dealer agreements for the following:

-	Determine compliance with the agreements.
-	Compare any recourse provisions to the bank's records.

7.	Review a list of dealer reserves. Ensure that any overdraft balances are paid within 30 days and any prepaid reserves are valued appropriately.

8.	Review the list of loans generated by brokers or finders and assess the quality of the loans. Consider:

- Whether the bank has obtained sufficient financial information to support the loans.
- The performance of the loans.
- What support is provided by credit enhancements, if any.

Asset Securitization

1. Determine whether the bank engages in asset securitization.

2. Review reports detailing each outstanding asset securitization and any in process.

3. Review securitization agreements. Evaluate:

- The significant terms of each securitization.
- Any practices that may create liability or recourse for the bank.

4. Evaluate the performance of each securitization by considering:

- Performance compared to the terms of the securitization.
- Significant trends in performance.

5. Through discussions with management, evaluate the collection policies applied to the securitized portfolio.

6. Evaluate the impact of collection programs, (such as granting extensions on problem loans), on performance reports to investors.

7. Determine whether the bank routinely repurchases past-due loans from the securitization. If there is a pattern of repurchases, investigate the recourse implications on the accounting treatment (i.e., whether the securitization is accounted for as a financing or sale).

8. If concerns are identified, refer to the "Asset Securitization" booklet for additional examination procedures.

Loans and Participations Purchased and Sold

1.	Review participation certificates and records, and determine that the parties share in the risks and contractual payments on a pro rata basis.

2.	Investigate any participations sold immediately prior to the examination to determine whether they were sold to avoid possible criticism during this examination.

Delinquent Loans and Repossessed Property

1.	Review key collection reports for delinquent loans and repossessed property that are used by management. Evaluate:

	•	Adequacy of the information.
	•	Collection activity, noting any changing conditions and adverse trends.

2.	Review the listings of delinquent loans (including renewals, extensions, and deferrals).

3.	Review the listings of repossessed personal property and determine that charge offs comply with bank policy and OCC guidelines.

4.	If loans and repossessions have not been charged off in accordance with policy guidelines, prepare a listing and discuss the accounts with management.

5.	Classify delinquent loans and repossessed property according to OCC guidelines.

6.	Review the key collection reports for delinquent loans and repossessed property that are used by management. Consider:

	•	Adequacy of the information.
	•	Collection activity, noting any changing conditions and adverse trends.

7.	Review any reports being submitted on delinquent and defaulted loans guaranteed by government agencies.

- Determine whether management is accurately informed and is complying with the reporting requirements.
- Determine that claims are being promptly filed after default.

8. Determine the extent to which renewals, extensions, and deferrals are used and the appropriateness of the volume.

Charge Offs

1. Review the schedule of voluntary charge offs made since the last examination. Consider:

   - For loans delinquent 120 days or more, review the bank's proof of past-due status.
   - For loans delinquent 90 to 120 days, review the bank's proof of past-due status and the reason for the charge off.

2. Prepare the charge-off form or IRS Express Determination Letter, if requested, for charge off of installment loans between examinations.

Concentrations of Credit

1. Coordinate with the examiner responsible for "Concentrations of Credit" to ensure that applicable procedures are performed.

Suspense Items

1. Review any loan debit and credit suspense items by identifying any large or stale items.

2. Discuss with management, and charge off the old items as appropriate.

Allowance for Loan and Lease Losses

1. Assess the adequacy of the ALLL provision for installment loans by using the most recent quarter-end data. Consider:

   - Whether management's allowance analysis is documented.
   - If the analysis properly recognizes the risks in the portfolio.
   - Whether the balance is an appropriate reflection of the inherent loss

in the installment portfolio.

2.   Forward the results of your analysis to the ALLL examiner.

Compliance with Laws and Regulations

Objective: To determine the level of compliance with applicable laws, rulings, and regulations relating to installment lending.

1.   If installment lending activities included screening potential loan customers, determine that screening policies comply with applicable consumer legislation, particularly anti-discrimination laws and regulations (refer to Banking Bulletin 91-50).

2.   Test compliance with the following laws, rulings, and regulations:

- 12 USC 84 and 12 CFR 32—Legal Lending Limits.
- 12 USC 375a, 12 CFR 215, and 12 USC 375b—Loans to Insiders.
- 12 CFR 2—Disposition of Credit Life Insurance Income.
- 31 CFR 103.33(a)—Financial Institution Records.
- 12 USC 371(c)—*Loans to Affiliates*.
- *18 USC 215—Commission or Gift for Procuring a Loan*.
- *2 USC 431(8)(B) and 2 USC 441b—Political Contributions and Loans*.
- 12 USC 1972—Tie-in Provisions.
- 12 USC 1972(2)—Loans to Insiders of Correspondent Banks.

3.   Determine if the consumer compliance examination uncovered any violations and whether corrective action was taken.

4.   If significant violations or exceptions were found, expand the test to:

- Evaluate subsequent compliance with any law or regulation where significant exceptions were identified internally.
- Determine that previously identified problems have been corrected.

Verification Procedures

Objective: Verify the bank's installment loans, and test the accuracy of the bank's records and adequacy of record keeping.

1. Identify any area with inadequate supervision and/or undue risk. Discuss with the bank EIC the need to perform expanded verification procedures as follows.

2. Test the additions of the trial balance and the reconciliation of the trial balance to the general ledger to determine whether the books and records properly reflect the bank's liability.

3. If verification procedures are considered necessary, use an appropriate sampling technique to select loans from the trial balance.

4. For sample loans to be verified, do the following:

    *   Check notes for completeness and agree date, amount, and terms, to the trial balance.
    *   For loans secured by negotiable collateral, check or confirm the collateral and hypothecation agreements with the holder.
    *   For loans secured by deposit accounts:
        -   Verify that interest rates on the account are in accordance with bank policy.
        -   Ensure accounts are checked for holds preventing unauthorized withdrawals.
    *   Verify that each file contains documentation supporting guarantees and subordination agreements, where appropriate.
    *   Determine that required insurance coverage is adequate and the bank is named as loss payee.
    *   Ensure that the number of payments made are:
        -   Based on note terms.
        -   Checked for accuracy to delinquent or current status and extension information.
        -   Agree with the trial balance.

5. For loans selected in above sample which were made or rewritten since the last examination, examine or review the following:

    *   Canceled check(s) to ensure the borrower's endorsement is the same as his or her signature on the note.
    *   Other endorsements on the check to determine the propriety of its final disposition.

- The bank's working papers to evaluate the disbursement of loan proceeds and ensure accuracy of payout calculations.

6.   If direct verification procedures are considered necessary, do the following:

   - Prepare and mail confirmation forms to borrowers (use balances as of the last billing date.) Consider:
     - Loans serviced by other institutions, either whole loans or participations, should be confirmed only with the servicing institution.
     - Loans serviced for other institutions, either whole loans or participations, should be confirmed with the buying institution and the borrower.
   - Confirmation forms should include the following:
     - Original amount of the loan.
     - The interest rate.
     - The current balance.
     - A brief description of the collateral supporting the loan.
   - After a reasonable time period, mail second requests to those borrowers who did not respond).
   - Follow up on any no-replies or exceptions and resolve differences with management.

7.   Obtain the installment loan unearned discount proration report and do the following:

   - Test the addition.
   - Agree the report total to the general ledger balance.

8.   Review and substantiate creditors' life, accident, and health insurance charges as follows:

   - Review the insurance policy contract and extract and disclose the monthly premium rate on working papers.
   - Compare the rate charged to the monthly premium computation form.
   - Compare the total amount of insured loans to the respective production list of insured loans.

- If the bank receives a commission, determine that the commission it received is appropriate.
- Account for all expenditures in the credit life insurance account since the preceding examination.
- Confirm, with the insurance company, any rebates or lack thereof received since the preceding examination.

9. Review late charges for accuracy and reasonableness by:

- Selecting a one-month time period since the preceding examination, and obtaining a schedule of late charges.
- Reviewing transaction journals for late charges added during the month.
- Tracing late charges collected to the appropriate income account in the general ledger.
- Ascertaining that reversals of late charges were properly approved.

10. Obtain a schedule of repossessed collateral sold since the previous examination.

11. Select, by an appropriate sampling technique, items for testing and determine:

- Sale prices, by referring to supporting documents such as sales invoices or receipts.
- The propriety of the entries made to record the sales, by:
  - Referring to published dealer wholesale values, condition reports, etc.
  - Evaluating any large expenditures made in connection with the sale of the item.
  - Confirming terms, conditions, and price with purchasers.

12. Obtain or prepare a schedule showing the monthly interest income amounts and the installment loan balances at each month end since the last examination and:

- Calculate or check yield.
- Investigate any significant fluctuations and/or trends.

13. If outside vendors are used for direct mail marketing efforts ensure that the bank regularly audits the vendor's controls and procedures.

Quality of Risk Management

Conclusion: The quality of risk management is (strong, satisfactory, weak).

Policy

Conclusion: The board (has/has not) established effective policies and standards governing installment lending activities.

Objective: To determine if the board of directors has adopted policies and underwriting standards for installment lending that are consistent with safe and sound banking practices and appropriate to the size of the bank and the nature and scope of its operations.

1. Determine whether the board of directors, consistent with its duties and responsibilities has adopted informal (unwritten) or formal (written) installment loan policies that establish:

    - Procedures for reviewing and approving installment loan applications.
    - Underwriting standards for each type of installment product offered.
    - Minimum documentation standards.

2. Review the adequacy of the bank's installment lending policy. Determine whether policy guidelines are satisfactory for the bank's installment loan operations in the following areas:

    - Acquisitions.
    - Operations.
    - Collections.
    - Renewals, extensions, and deferral programs.
    - Indirect Lending.
    - Asset Securitization.
    - ALLL provision for the installment loan portfolio.

3. Determine whether the board approves installment lending policies annually and whether they evaluate existing installment loan policies to determine if they are compatible with changing market conditions and laws and regulations.

4. Review the bank's underwriting standards as outlined in its board-

---

approved policy and evaluate:

- The adequacy and reasonableness of underwriting guidelines.
- Whether the standards recognize the risks associated with installment lending, including credit, operational, and legal risks.
- The sufficiency of guidelines provided to staff (for example, whether the parameters for accepting or rejecting risk are well-delineated).
- Whether loan credit limits and loan officer approvals are reasonable.
- Guidelines for renewals and extensions.

5.   Determine whether collection policies have been established that address the following:

- Delinquent notices are sent before the loan becomes 30 days past due.
- Collection efforts are intensified when a loan becomes two payments past due.
- Records of collection efforts are maintained in the customer's credit or electronic file.
- Field or outside collectors are under the supervision of an officer and the collectors are required to submit progress reports.
- All collections are acknowledged.
- All documents held outside the regular files, pertaining to installment loans under collection, are evidenced by a transmittal sheet and receipt.
- Delinquency lists are generated on a timely basis (indicate frequency).

Processes

Conclusion: Processes and practices governing how the bank will pursue its installment lending objectives (are/are not) effective.

Objective: To determine if processes, including internal controls, are adequate and consistent with prudent underwriting practices.

Management

1. Depending on the size and complexity of operations and types of loans extended, assess the efficiency and effectiveness of the bank's installment lending operations, (including installment acquisition, loan operation and collection functions). Consider:

   - How loans acquisitions are managed, including:
     - Marketing.
     - Loan origination.
     - Types of loan approval processes:
       - Judgmental method.
       - Credit scoring models.
   - How installment loan operations are managed, including:
     - Processing the loan after approval.
     - Disbursing loan proceeds.
     - Preparing payment books or monthly statements.
     - Managing collateral and documentation.
     - Preparing various reports (delinquencies, extensions, renewals, and irregular payments).
   - How the collection process is managed, including:
     - Handling delinquent borrowers.
     - Repossessing collateral.
     - Disposing of repossessions.

2. Evaluate management's process for periodically revising policies and procedures. Consider:

   - Whether the process is effective in terms of incorporating necessary and timely changes.
   - What method is used to communicate policies and procedures to the staff.
   - Through discussions with staff members, evaluate the effectiveness and timeliness of the communication system.

3. If applicable, determine credit administration's role in formulating policy, monitoring compliance with policy, and monitoring lending practices and portfolio quality.

4. Evaluate the system to ensure compliance with underwriting standards for reasonableness.

---

5. Evaluate management's process for ensuring that new loan quality is consistent with policy and the board's capacity and tolerance for risk. Consider:

    - Any significant changes in credit criteria and terms.
    - If credit scoring is used, compare portfolio distribution by credit score as of this examination date to prior periods.

6. If credit scoring is used as a method for loan approval, evaluate how management uses credit scoring as a means to track the portfolio and manage risk. Consider the following:

    - Portfolio distribution.
    - Delinquency distribution.
    - Reasons for override exceptions.

Indirect Lending

1. Evaluate the procedures used to purchase loans generated by dealers.

2. Assess the adequacy of the bank's risk management process(es) for its dealer relationships and discuss any concerns with management.

3. Determine whether the bank exercises similar controls over indirect lending operations as they do for loans in their own portfolio. Consider:

    - Are separate controls maintained, or easily generated, to include loans originated by dealers?
    - Are payments made directly to the bank and not through the dealer?
    - Are dealer lines reaffirmed at least annually?
    - Are required documents on file in connection with the establishment of each dealer line?
    - Are signed extension agreements obtained from dealers before extending accounts originally discounted on a repurchase agreement or other recourse basis?
    - Are checks made to see that down payment amounts do not misrepresent the sales price?
    - Are procedures in place to prevent the dealer from making payments

to disguise a delinquent account?

- Do prohibitions exist preventing the bank from bringing loans current by charges to a dealer's reserve accounts?
- Are selling prices, as listed by the dealer, verified?
- Are overdrafts prohibited in the dealer reserve and holdback accounts?
- Are procedures in effect to have the title application controlled by someone other than the purchaser?
- Are credit checks on borrowers performed independently of the dealer, or are the dealer's credit checks independently verified?

Acquisitions

1. Evaluate management's acquisition process by considering the following:

- New Product Development:
  - Are appropriate feasibility studies performed prior to product implementation?
  - Does credit administration have an appropriate role in the developmental process, and does their role effectively promote sound underwriting?
  - Do controls exist to ensure that compliance and underwriting issues are incorporated into all new products?
  - Does a review and approval process exist to ensure that all necessary participants are involved in product development prior to implementation?
  - Does the planning process require research and adequate MIS support for product supervision and administration (such systems should be operational prior to product implementation)?
- Marketing Plans:
  - Is the data used to develop the plans appropriate?
  - Are market, economic, or profitability studies prepared either externally or internally?
  - Are plans developed and implemented, noting time frames for activities and the approval process (who approves and when)?
  - Are risks (credit, interest rate, transaction, compliance, strategic, and reputation) sufficiently addressed in the plans?
  - Do plans incorporate a loosening or tightening of credit standards?
  - Do plans adequately address the stated direction and goals of the installment lending department and the bank as a whole?

- Credit criteria used for preapproved loans:
  - Have preapproved programs been adequately "tested" before the bank engaged in any large scale credit offering.
  - Do controls, including audits performed, ensure that preapproved offers are consistent with credit criteria.

Asset Securitization

1. Evaluate the process the bank uses to establish its accounting treatment for securitized loans.

2. Discuss with management their plans for ensuring the bank has adequate systems for servicing the current and anticipated securitization.

Collections

1. Review the adequacy of procedures governing the collection area.

2. If automated collection systems are used, assess the systems' strengths and limitations. Consider:

   - If the systems interface with each other.
   - The adequacy of key MIS reports produced by each system.

3. Review management's collection strategies by determining:

   - How strategies are established.
   - How they measures the effectiveness of their strategies.

Repossessions

1. Determine if procedures have been established to ensure that:

   - Management takes timely action to receive full advantage of any dealer endorsement or repurchase agreement.
   - Any notice of intention to sell is mailed to all parties liable on the account.
   - Bids are required before the sale of the item.
   - Bids are retained in the borrower's credit file.

- Open repossessions are physically checked on a monthly basis.
- Surplus funds received from the sale of a repossession are mailed back to the borrower in the form of a cashier's check.
- Any deficiency balance remains after the sale of the repossession is charged off.
- The bill of sale is properly completed and signed by an officer.
- Separate general ledger control is maintained.

Loan Operations

1. Determine whether adequate processes have been implemented to ensure the accuracy of bank records in the following areas:

   Subsidiary Loan Records
   - Is the preparation and posting of subsidiary loan records performed or adequately reviewed by persons who do not also issue:
     - official checks or drafts singly?
     - handle cash?
   - Are subsidiary loan records reconciled daily to the appropriate general ledger accounts?
   - Are reconciling items investigated by persons who do not also handle cash?
   - Are delinquent account collection requests and past-due notices:
     - Checked to trial balances used in reconciling installment loan subsidiary records to general ledger accounts?
     - Handled only by persons who do not also handle cash?
   - Are inquiries about loan balances investigated by persons who do not also handle cash?
   - Are documents supporting recorded credit adjustments checked or tested subsequently by persons who do not also handle cash. (If so, explain briefly.)
   - Is a daily record maintained summarizing loan transaction details, (i.e., loans made, payments received, and interest collected) to support applicable general ledger account entries?
   - Are frequent note and liability ledger trial balances prepared and reconciled with controlling accounts by employees who do not process or record loan transactions?
   - Are two authorized signatures required to effect a status change in an individual customer account?

- Is an exception report produced and reviewed by management that includes extensions, rewrites, renewals, or any factors that would result in a change in customer account status?
- Do customer account records clearly indicate accounts that have been renewed, rewritten, or extended?
- Are subsidiary payment records and files pertaining to serviced loans segregated and identifiable?

Loan Interest
- Is the preparation and posting of interest records performed or reviewed by persons who do not also:
  - Issue official checks or drafts singly?
  - Handle cash?
- Are independent interest computations made and compared, or adequately tested, to initial interest records by persons who do not also:
  - Issue official checks or drafts singly?
  - Handle cash?

Collateral
- Are multicopy, pre-numbered records maintained that:
  - Detail the complete description of collateral pledged?
  - Are typed or completed in ink?
  - Are signed by the customer?
- Are receipts issued to customers that cover each item of negotiable collateral deposited with the bank?
- Are the receipt and release of collateral to borrowers and the recording of entries in the collateral register, performed by different employees?
- Is negotiable collateral held under joint custody?
- Is all collateral for a single loan maintained in a separate file?
- Are receipts obtained and filed for released collateral?
- Are records maintained of any entry to the collateral vault?
- Are controls in effect on collateral to ensure that:
  - The bank's own deposits held as collateral are noted on the deposit trial balance?
  - Descriptions of motor vehicles, as set forth on the certificate of title and insurance policies, are checked to the chattel mortgages

or other appropriate documents granting security interest in the vehicle?
- An insurance maturity tickler file is maintained?
- Procedures are in effect to make sure single interest insurance coverage is obtained in case regular insurance is canceled or expires?
- All insurance policies on file includes a loss payable clause in favor of the bank?
- Filings are made on all security agreements?
- When a judgment action is returned involving real property, supporting lien searches and property appraisals are performed?
- Are control records maintained that identify loans secured by junior liens on real estate?
- Do records indicate the current balance for loans secured by superior liens on the same property?

Personnel

Conclusion: Management (does/does not) have the skills and knowledge necessary to manage the risk inherent in installment lending.

Objective: To determine management's ability to conduct residential and home equity lending in a safe and sound manner.

1. Through discussions with management, ascertain their knowledge of current policies and procedures.

2. Review the organizational chart in conjunction with management resumes, to assess the overall structure and managerial experience of significant installment lending department personnel. If no chart is available, discuss structure and experience with department management.

3. Review management-prepared staffing analyses for the installment lending area to determine adequacy.

4. Evaluate whether staffing levels are appropriate considering present and future plans.

5. Based on the results of the quantity and quality of risk procedures, assess the level of competency of significant personnel involved in the installment lending functions.

6. Assess the adequacy of collection staffing by considering the following:

   - Experience levels of collectors and supervisors.
   - Staff turnover.
   - Ratio of accounts to collectors.
   - Ratio of collectors to supervisors.
   - Delinquency levels and trends.
   - Portfolio growth.

7. Using management reports or the UBPR, review management's performance by evaluating the following:

   - Profitability trends.
   - Delinquency trends.
   - Loss and recovery trends.

Controls

Conclusion: The control systems used to measure performance, make decisions, and assess effectiveness of existing processes (are/are not) effective.

Objective: Determine the adequacy of control systems used to monitor installment lending activities.

1. Evaluate the methods and information management uses to monitor installment loan portfolio quality.

2. Evaluate the controls management uses to monitor new loan volume, and whether the quality of new loans is consistent with policy and the bank's capacity and tolerance for risks.

3. Determine whether loan review or internal audit reviews loans for credit quality and whether they form a conclusion as to the quality of the underwriting, the strength of the portfolio, and the effectiveness of

controls.

4.   Evaluate the effectiveness of the loan review system and/or audit function in identifying risk in installment lending. Consider:

   • Scope and coverage of review(s).
   • Frequency of reviews.
   • Qualifications of loan review and audit personnel.
   • Comprehensiveness and accuracy of findings.
   • Adequacy and timeliness of follow up.

5.   Review loan review and audit reports, and management's responses to criticisms and determine whether management instituted adequate corrective actions to address audit recommendations.

6.   Make a judgement as to the effectiveness of the loan review process and/or internal audit and document the analysis.

7.   Evaluate the adequacy of the monthly MIS package used by senior management to monitor the installment loan portfolio. Consider:

   • Whether the reports include adequate information on the quality and volume of new loans and the overall quality of the installment loan portfolio by type of product.
   • Whether reports are used to monitor levels and trends in renewals, extensions, delinquencies, repossessions, losses, and recoveries.
   • If reports are generated of loans by loan officer to determine any negative trends.
   • If used as a management tool, evaluate dynamic delinquency or vintage analysis reports to compare the performance of loans booked in different periods (quarterly, or monthly, if volume is sufficient) for equal amounts of time.

8.   Determine whether the MIS used in installment lending provides management with sufficient information to monitor the quality of credit underwriting.

9.   Evaluate the adequacy of MIS for asset securitization at both the board and management levels.

10. Assess the adequacy of controls used to ensure all necessary parties review changes to existing installment loan policies, prior to their final adoption.

11. Evaluate the bank's internal control review system to ensure the following controls exist:

- Duties are properly segregated and loan officers are prohibited from processing loan payments.
- The amount of credit life and accident and health insurance on new loans is recomputed.
- The amount of discount on new loans is recomputed.
- Rebates on prepaid loans are recomputed.
- Daily transactions are checked to subsequent general ledger postings.
- New loan documentation is reviewed.
- All information contained in reports that are submitted to the board of directors or any committee are reviewed for errors or omissions.
- A periodic review of income accruals is conducted for accuracy.
- Unearned discount or income account entries are reviewed.
- All charged off loans are reviewed for proper approval.
- Charged off notes are periodically reconciled to the control ledger.
- The dealer's reserve and holdback agreements are reviewed periodically to determine the adequacy of the balances in the deposit account.
- Dealer reserve balances are periodically verified.
- Payments are accurately and promptly posted.
- The collection or reversal of late charges is periodically reviewed.
- That extension fees are collected on all extended loans.
- That discounted dealer paper is properly endorsed and within established guidelines.
- The installment loan portfolio is in compliance with laws and regulations.
- Trial balance reconcilements are compared to the general ledger.

Conclusion

Objective: Determine overall conclusions and communicate examination findings regarding the quantity of risk and quality of risk management systems in installment lending operations.

Objective: Initiate corrective action when policies, practices, procedures, or control systems are deficient or when violations of law, rulings, or regulations have been noted.

1. Prepare a memorandum to the EIC or examiner assigned "Loan Portfolio Management" regarding:

    - The quality of department management.
    - Quantity of risk. Consider:
      - Credit quality and collectability of the portfolio, including trends in outstandings, delinquencies, and losses.
      - Compliance with established guidelines.
      - Compliance with applicable laws, rulings, and regulations.
      - The quality of loan underwriting practices.
    - Quality of risk management. Consider:
      - Adequacy of policies and underwriting standards.
      - Adequacy of processes, including planning.
      - Management's ability to conduct installment lending in a safe and sound manner.
      - Adequacy of control systems, including loan review, audit, and management information systems.
    - Any concerns and/or recommendations regarding the condition of the department including:
      - Root causes of problems.
      - Factors contributing to any less than satisfactory conditions.
    - Adverse trends within the installment lending department.
    - The accuracy and completeness of the bank's MIS reports.
    - Internal control deficiencies or exceptions.
    - The adequacy of departmental planning, including projected growth areas.
    - Violations of laws, rulings, and regulations.
    - Summary financial information including:
      - Delinquent loans, segregating those considered "A" paper.
      - Loans not supported by current and complete financial

information.
- Loans on which collateral documentation is deficient.
- Concentrations of credit.
- Special mention and classified loans.
- Management's strategies to correct noted deficiencies.

2. Determine the impact on the aggregate and direction of risk assessments for any applicable risks identified by performing the above procedures. Examiners should refer to guidance provided under the OCC's large and community bank risk assessment programs.

- Risk Categories: Compliance, Credit, Interest Rate, Liquidity, Reputation, Strategic, Transaction
- Risk Conclusions: High, Moderate, or Low
- Risk Direction: Increasing, Stable, or Decreasing

3. Determine in consultation with the EIC, if the risks identified are significant enough to merit bringing them to the board's attention in the report of examination. If so, prepare items for inclusion under the headings Matters Requiring Board Attention.

- MRBA should cover practices that:
  - Deviate from sound fundamental principles and are likely to result in financial deterioration if not addressed
  - Result in substantive noncompliance with laws.
- MRBA should discuss:
  - Causative factors contributing to the problem
  - Consequences of inaction
  - Management's commitment for corrective action
  - The time frame and person(s) responsible for corrective action.

4. Discuss findings with management including conclusions regarding applicable risks.

5. As appropriate, prepare a brief installment lending comment for inclusion in the report of examination.

6. Provide either the examiner assigned LPM or the bank EIC with a memorandum specifically stating what the OCC needs to do in the future

to effectively supervise installment lending in this bank. Include supervisory objectives, timing of activities, staffing requirements, and estimates of workdays required.

7. Prepare a memorandum or update the work program with any information that will facilitate future examinations.

8. Update the OCC's Electronic Information System and any applicable report of examination schedules or tables.

9. Organize and reference working papers in accordance with OCC guidance.